*A Kingdom Woman's Guide to Fruitful Time Management*

# It's About TIME

BETTYE
McCASKILL
BRIDGES

**IT'S ABOUT TIME: A Kingdom Woman's Guide to Fruitful Time Management**
*by Bettye McCaskill Bridges*

Copyright © 2020 Bettye McCaskill Bridges

All rights reserved. No part of this publication may be reproduced, stored in a retrieval system, or transmitted in any form by means of electronic, mechanical, photocopying, recording, or otherwise, except for the inclusion of brief quotations in a review, without prior permission in writing from the author and publisher.

*Unless otherwise noted, Scripture quotations contained herein are taken from the King James Version, Public Domain*

*Scripture quotations marked (NKJV) are taken from the <u>New King James Version</u>®. Copyright © 1982 by Thomas Nelson. Used by permission. All rights reserved..*

*Scripture quotations marked (AKJV) are taken from the <u>American King James Version</u>, Public Domain.*

*Scripture quotations marked (NIV) are taken from the <u>Holy Bible, New International Version</u>®, NIV®. Copyright ©1973, 1978, 1984, 2011 by Biblica, Inc.™ Used by permission of Zondervan. All rights reserved worldwide.*

*Scripture quotations marked (AMPC) are taken from <u>Amplified Bible, Classic Edition</u>, copyright © 1954, 1958, 1962, 1964, 1965, 1987 by The Lockman Foundation.*

**CONTACT THE AUTHOR:** bettye.bridges@yahoo.com

**FRONT COVER PHOTO CREDIT:** Greg Anthony Photography.

Book Design by Shannon Crowley
Treasure Image & Publishing—TreasureImagePublishing.com

Edited by Dr. Mary Edwards
Leaves of Gold Consulting, LLC—LeavesOfGoldConsulting.com

*EDITOR'S DISCLAIMER:*
*Author is responsible to confirm the accuracy of all scripture references.*

# DEDICATION

This book is dedicated to the memory of my late mother, Maezell Topps McCaskill, and my children, Brandi Bridges Wheeler and Gerald Andrew Bridges.

Thank you for always pushing me to do and BE more! I love you guys more than you will ever know.

To GOD be the Glory!

# ACKNOWLEDGEMENTS

I would like to acknowledge a few very special people who encouraged me along the way to write this book. First, my Pastor, Dr. James L. Morman and his wife Sister Loretta Morman. They assigned me to teach a 12-week, one-hour class on "Fruitful Time Management," where the idea for this book was born.

Two very good friends and mentor National Sales Director Emeritus, Joyce Z. Grody, and Sister Beatrice Smith, founder of God Almighty Christian Community Services. Dr. Mary Edwards, my coach, editor and a very successful author in her own right. My former office assistant and friend, Valerie Stokes, for her ability to take my scribbles and put them in perfect order.

# FOREWORD

I am Godly proud of my daughter in the faith who was obedient to her call to publish a book that will transform the lives of men and women.

Tackling such a topic such as Time Management is timeless and relatable, in that we all--at some point in our lives-- have needed help managing the many responsibilities we have.

You'll soon learn in this book how a teaching assignment for our ministry (CTAB Church) led to the creation of this book. I'm grateful to serve as the leader and Pastor of those who are obedient to the word of God and who seek God ON purpose, FOR their purpose. Glory to God!

Many are familiar with **Ecclesiastes 3:1 (KJV)** *"To every thing there is a season, and a time to every purpose under the heaven."*

God has given us 24 hours in each day, yet many of us get lost in being overburdened, ill prepared, and undisciplined to handle the tasks at hand. In the busyness of our days, there are some who forget to set the tone during communication with the Heavenly Father.

Bettye reminds us in this book how time with God is of the utmost importance as we carryout mundane or sometimes tedious tasks. He is the only one who sees our beginning and our end, knowing that what we do with the time between determines the success of each day and the potential gratification we shall feel once our life has ended and we reach the kingdom of heaven—yearning for that hopeful phrase to be uttered, *well done.*

**Dr. James L. Morman**
**Pastor of Christian Tabernacle Church**
**Southfield, Michigan**

# INTRODUCTION

As Christians, we ought not manage our time the same way as the world. We must make sure that we seek God in everything that we do. We are to organize our time and plan wisely for the future. I have a plaque that says, "Don't count your blessings, but make your blessings count."

A very real blessing to me now is the Leadership of my pastor, Dr. James L. Morman and his wife, Sister Loretta Morman, of Christian Tabernacle Church, Southfield, Michigan. I was assigned last Spring to teach a 12-week course titled "Fruitful Time Management." I was willing, of course, but I asked the minister who relayed the assignment to me if they had an outline or lesson plan for the topic. His response was, "I will check."

The next day he said, "No, Sister Bridges. You are to provide the outline and pastor wants it a month before the class begins."

I was honored to be asked but was a bit unsure if I could put it together. However, I set out doing my research, prepared, taught the class and it was great. The members were so gracious and said that it helped them and it certainly blessed me, as I learned from them as well.

This project is and has been such a blessing. Therefore, I want to share my journey of learning the importance of being "fruitful" as I served God, raised my family and built my business in the process. Nothing is impossible with God!

Another major blessing in my life was being introduced to Mary Kay Cosmetics in my mid 20's. I was going to literally "change the world," because I knew that God had a call on my life and I thought it was to be in business for myself.

Actually, that was true. I believe God used Mary Kay Cosmetics to prepare me for the life He had for me, and for that I am truly grateful. I share that because many of you may "think" you know what God has called you to and find out along the way that the very thing you are running from is what you are actually called to do!

*Many plans are in a man's mind, but it is the*
*Lord's purpose for him that will stand.*
PROVERBS 19:21 (AMPC)

Just for clarity sake, when the Bible says man—it's mankind—so that includes us too, ladies. This passage will become even more clear and important as you go along.

Also, Mary Kay Ash, the Founder of Mary Kay Cosmetics, who was a mentor to me as well (I will share more about that as we continue), had a saying that stuck with me and always reminded me of that scripture—although we can "plan" what we want to do, God always had the final say. Her quote was, "Life is what happens to you while you're planning something else." Let that sink in for a minute; maybe ponder it!

My prayer is that you will ponder many things in this book, so that it will sincerely bring "change" in a positive way for your life. That positive way will empower you to become "fruitful." It's About Time!

# TABLE OF CONTENTS

# CHAPTER ONE

# Make Time for God and You Every Day!

*As for me, I call to God, and the Lord saves me. Evening, morning and noon I cry out in distress, and he hears my voice.*
Psalm 55:16-17 (niv)

We must assume personal responsibility for use of our time. We are encouraged to "redeem the time," which means to make the most of the time God has given us (Ephesians 5:16).

We make personal choices daily on how we will spend our time. Later, in Chapter 3, I share a Weekly Plan Sheet with suggestions on how to be the most productive (fruitful) with the time you have.

This book is to be a suggestion, as each person reading has different obligations, goals, lifestyles, family size and commitments. You will be the final decision maker as to how your time is spent; I will guide you to the most advantageous ways based on your personal desires.

As a Kingdom Woman, putting God first will empower you to perform in every area of your life, therefore being able to get the most important things done on a daily basis (**Six Most Important Things List**). Make a plan that includes daily private time. This is a MUST to be sincerely <u>fruitful</u> in our daily lives. Then plan times for you; self-care is something that was missing in my mother's generation. Therefore, in my case personally, I spent time taking care of the children, working and serving. I let myself get lost in the process.

This is why it's so important to actually PLAN time for YOU! We'll talk more about how this is done in Chapter 2 and 3.

When your daily plan begins with private time with God, you are in His will for your life.

*For we are His workmanship, created in*
*Christ Jesus for good works, which God*
*prepared beforehand*
*that we should walk in them.*
EPHESIANS 2:10 (NKJV)

This way you are not being limited to just your work or in ministry, but God will guide you in your recreational life and your friendships. This giving you varied opportunities to be a witness in all that you do.

Each night before you go to bed, spend 5-10 minutes jotting down the "Most Important Things" you need/want to get done the next day. This is a two-fold advantage: it assures you won't forget important things AND you will have a more restful, peaceful sleep. As a matter of fact, keep a note pad and pen next to your bed, because you'd be surprised at what comes to mind as soon as your head hits the pillow! You'll be delighted when you can just jot it down and not have to think about it anymore.

Close each day with a quick prayer. One that you read that is scripture based, if you just can't think. There will be times that your days have been so filled and fast-paced that one more "thought" is too much.

**Pivotal Points**: Carve out 5-15 minutes, three times daily, to pray, seek the Lord and ask for guidance and discernment. NO MATTER how busy you are. This is part of your self-care. (We will talk more about that in Chapter 7.)

You may not be able to get on your knees three times per day but, trust me, God will meet you when you make time for Him.

# CHAPTER TWO

# Make the Most of Your Mornings

*And in the morning, rising up a great while
before day, he went out, and departed into a
solitary place, and there prayed.*
MARK 1:35 (AKJV)

Because this book is for ANYONE desiring to make better use of time, whatever schedule you have to deal with—wherever you are—if you're working a second or third shift now while building on your dream—your <u>morning</u> in this case are your first waking hours of the day.

If you are currently working a full-time job, while raising a family, and pursuing a different dream your "day job" is your disciplinarian, because for now it keeps you on track. By that I mean, you know what you have to do from 8-4 or 9-5, etc. This makes it all the more important to PLAN your time.

## <u>Six Most Important Things IDEA</u>
### <u>*(Ivy Lee by way of Charles Schwab)*</u>

During my career with Mary Kay Cosmetics, I learned of the **Six Most Important Things List.** Mary Kay Ash, herself, shared this very powerful, but simple concept that was taught by a consultant named Ivy Lee who was hired by Charles Schwab during the time he was head of Bethlehem Steel Corporation.

Lee offered to increase the productivity of Schwab's people and he would let him decide what the results were worth. After a few months of seeing results, Schwab sent Lee a check for $35,000—that was in the early 1900's; by today's dollar that would be over $70,000!!!

In her book, *"Miracles Happen,"* by Mary Kay Ash, Chapter 10 is entitled "The $35,000 List." This is where I first learned about the six most important things.

**_Here is how it works_:**

At the end of each working day, write down a list of the **Six Most Important Things** that you need to accomplish tomorrow. Stick to **only six** items.

Organize these tasks in order of importance (their actual importance and not just how easy they are).

The next day, focus on the first task only. Only move on to the second task when the first task is completed.

Continue like this until you've reached the end of your day. Add any remaining items to a new list of **six most important** tasks for the next day.

Repeat every working day.

This works because it forces you to actually get started on completing your task list. It enables you to stay on track by sticking to your priorities and simply moving them along your timelines as necessary.

# CHAPTER THREE

# Plan Your Days— Be Intentional

*Commit thy works unto the Lord, and thy thoughts (plans) shall be established.*
PROVERBS 16:3

## The Five P's: Proper Planning Prevents Poor Performance

To complement the **Six Most Important Things List** will be your personal **Weekly Plan Sheet.** (See example at the end of this Chapter). In order to be intentional, we are to learn to prioritize and put the most important things first.

This way less important things have to "fight" their way into your schedule, and trust me they will.

I read an article, while researching for my class, on fruitful time management from Desiring God.org and the Executive Editor of that website, David Mathis said (in the article) "Plan with big stones—our little pebbles are the smaller things to which we regularly give time but don't contribute to the main priorities."

This is where proper planning comes in and the critical use of the **Weekly Plan Sheet.**

This sheet is your personal schedule of how you'll get the **Six Most Important Things** done "daily" on a weekly basis.

These are life lessons I learned along the way, as I branched out from my traditional teaching profession (and calling) to become an Independent Business Owner in the world of Direct Sales.

I was married, working full-time, raising two children and working heavily in my church for a span of 10 years, 1992–2002.

I look back over those years and I am truly grateful for the teachings of Mary Kay Ash for the **Six Most Important Things List** and the **Weekly Plan Sheet**, otherwise I'm not sure I would have been able to achieve all that I did—Prioritizing is/was the Key! (In 1995 we qualified for our first Pink Cadillac and I was able to leave my teaching job to pursue my business full-time)

As you make your plan, I suggest Saturday or Sunday evening check with ALL family members.

On your **Plan Sheet**, record ALL of the commitments you must attend to during the week; children may forget their school meetings, parent/teacher conferences, etc.

If you are married, you guys may want to consider a "date night" (or day, depending on your schedules). If it is not on the sheet, it usually does not get done! You may have to take that stance once or twice to let your family and friends know that while your love is unconditional, your time is not.

This may sound too regimented, however, as the saying goes, "People really don't plan to fail, they FAIL to PLAN."

Here is a blank **Weekly Plan Sheet.** Take the time to do an "ideal" weekly plan. Begin with your uprising; start with your quiet time with God—preferably before you wake the rest of the family.

This is a learning process—if you are unmarried or single with no children, it is a great time to practice this habit.

Habits make us and, if you already have the habit of planning BEFORE you are married or a wife and mother, you're getting ahead of the game.

Mary Kay used to say, "It's better to be a 'glad I did' rather than a 'wish I had' person any day."

YOU are doing the planning, so remember to MAKE time for God and you.

# WEEKLY PLAN SHEET

*Download printable sheet at http://bit.do/WeeklyPlanSheet*

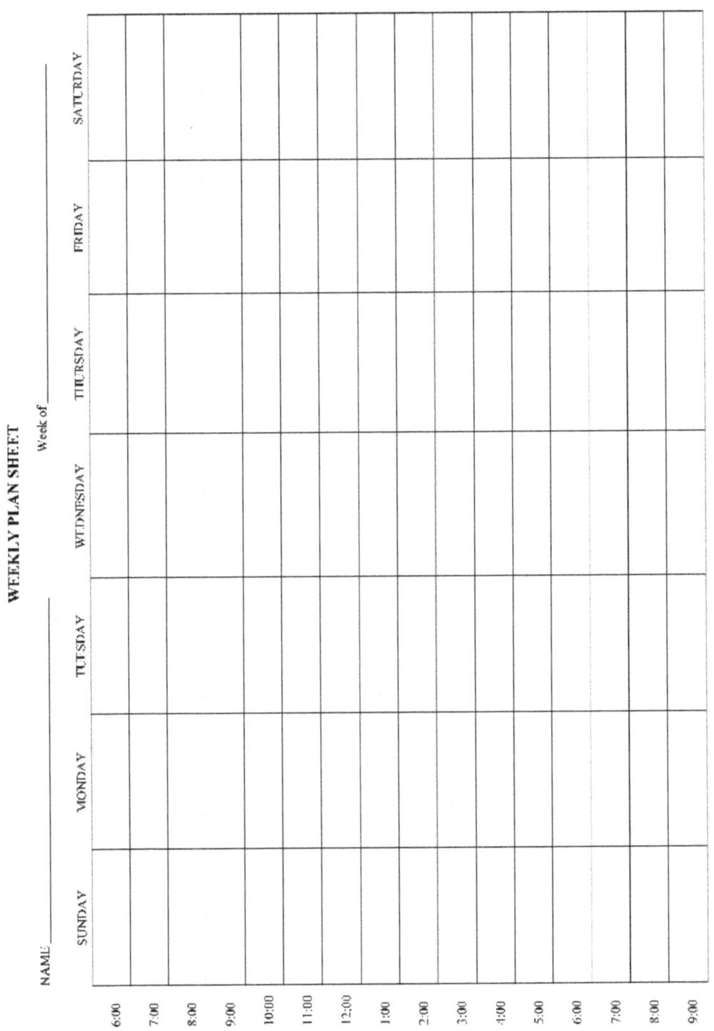


For more information, please contact
Bettye M. Bridges at NSD2004@gmail.com

# CHAPTER FOUR

# Seek Wisdom from God

*If any of you lack wisdom, let him ask of God,*
*that giveth to all men (mankind) liberally,*
*and upbraideth not; and it shall be given him.*
JAMES 1:5

Many people confuse knowledge with wisdom. Let me be very clear: knowledge is simply the acquisition of information. It has been said, "Knowledge is knowing <u>what to do</u>," Wisdom is <u>doing it</u>! Therefore, wisdom from God may be further knowing, WHAT to do WHEN!

Many years ago, I saw a sign that read: "Knowledge is a poor man's wealth."

I literally had to ponder that statement. Not because I didn't understand what it said, but because all of my life I had heard, "Knowledge is Power!" I submit to you today that we have been sold a "bill of goods" in that phrase. Knowledge alone is <u>NOT</u> power, but the <u>application</u> of that knowledge is where that power lies!

Therefore, I beseech you to apply the knowledge you receive from this book as you read and gain knowledge about Mastering You! I have learned that we are the greatest challenge we've got!

So you want to be mindful to "master you:" your emotions, thoughts and actions. Your emotions drive your thoughts and your thoughts control your actions.

Distractions come sometimes to take us off course. You must pray for the wisdom to know something is attempting to destroy your goal or objective or if you are to pivot totally or just temporarily.

With this in mind, I encourage you to be careful of the 4 D's. Distractions come in many ways. However, we must be careful how we allow them to control our time. We must pray earnestly for guidance as to what is important and MUST be done now or what may be a distraction just to destroy whatever we are doing in the name of Jesus or for His sake!

## The Four D's

1.  **Distraction:** usually comes to throw us off or redirect our plans

2.  **Delay:** If we allow ourselves to be delayed too long we may never reach our goals

3.  **Discouraged:** we have all heard that discouragement is one of the greatest tools of the enemy, so if we stay in that mode too long we can be (notice I used "can be" because you have a choice.

Hallelujah!). Fight discouragement with ACTION

4.   **Destroyed:** here we lose our VISION and forget what our dreams & goals are!

**Be very mindful of Distractions and procrastination!**

**REMEMBER THE 4 D'S**

**DISTRACTION leads to DELAY leads to DISCOURAGEMENT leads to DESTRUCTION**

# CHAPTER FIVE

# **Live with Eternity in Mind**

*While we look not at the things which are seen, but at the things which are not seen: for the things which are seen are temporal (brief and fleeting); but the things which are not seen are eternal (everlasting).*
II CORINTHIANS 4:18

We are to continually meditate on scripture and allow the Lord to direct our lives. Everything in this life will burn. Don't put your focus on the world. Secure your vision for the future *(see Ecclesiastes 3:11 and II Corinthians 5:6-10).*

Our perspective on the future impacts our decisions in the present. My mother used to say, "Don't let what people say and how they act bother you. You want to please God. These people don't have a heaven or hell to put you in." As I matured in life and actually studied the Word for myself, I came to understand, "Only what you do for Christ will last."

While this is a paraphrasing of the scripture itself in II Corinthians referenced, the message behind the verse is that we, as believers, should focus on pleasing the Lord, realizing that there is no eternal value in the things of the world.

So, when planning and prioritizing your time for the most "fruitful" or productive outcome, think about what you're really going to gain by spending your precious time on something that's not going to bring glory to God or advance your career/goal, bless you or your family.

This Chapter is one I recommend reading and re-reading or pondering, because it will require a different type of maturity in your spiritual walk to stay focused on your "eternal benefits."

## <u>To Strengthen Your Relationship with God</u>

Philippians 4:6-7—Be careful

I Peter 5:6-7—Humble yourselves therefore…

John 14:27—Peace I leave with you, my peace

Psalm 34:17-19—The righteous cry and the

Isaiah 40:31—But they that wait

Deuteronomy 31:6—Be strong in God

Psalm 112:6-8—Surely

II Timothy 1:7—God doesn't give us
the spirit of fear

The most powerful word one can learn is a simple, "no." It is very challenging to learn to say "no," when you really want to assist someone, or be a help. However, you cannot always say, "yes," when you become over-committed and wear yourself thin. When you do not make time for God and yourself, in the long run you are setting yourself up for failure.

Remember Matthew 6:33a, *"seek ye first the Kingdom of God …"* there are commitments that you will have in different stages in your life that will allow you to be who God called you to be and when you seek God first, He will guide and direct you.

I did not always follow this teaching, which is why I can share with you what the outcome and/or challenges will be. It is my desire that you learn from my mistakes (rather than make them). Wouldn't it be great if you were able to avoid as many pitfalls as possible?

# CHAPTER SIX

# Develop a Great Work Ethic

*In all labor there is profit, but the talk of the lips tendeth only to penury.*
PROVERBS 14:23

Please do not treat this book as if you're a student in school to be read, memorized and then never used. This is to be <u>interactive</u>. This is "self-help." Use wisdom to apply the knowledge you receive here. Just knowing this (retaining information) is not enough, but application is the key. Part B of that scripture in the Amplified Bible version says "But idle talk leads only to poverty."

By now, you are keenly aware (if you weren't when you began) that being conscious of time and understanding that we each have the same 24 hours in a day speaks volumes to the fact that it's not how much time you have, but what you CHOOSE to do with your time, that makes all the difference.

My recommendation to you is to work <u>smart</u>!

Mary Kay taught us many powerful admonitions. One very impactful to me was, "Don't spend dollar time on penny jobs." I read those words very early in my career with Mary Kay. I worked that business in all the ways anyone could.

By that I mean I worked it as a single person, a single mom and married with children. In all those forms, there was one thing consistent—I had to use my time wisely.

One of the reasons I feel led to share my story about time and how to be "fruitful" is because I literally "failed forward" to the successes I enjoy. I made many mistakes along the way and my desire is that you can learn from my mistakes and be able to empower yourself at whatever level you are.

I am a doer; always have been and prayerfully always will be. Being raised under the teaching, *"To whom much is given, much is required,"* (Luke 12:48B) it seems I was always put in positions to do much more than I thought I was capable of doing. About two years after attaining the highest position available in Mary Kay—National Sales Director—I was privileged to have a mentoring session at Corporate with the head of my Division at the time and the head of Sales Education and Motivation at the time.

During that session, I learned what "defining moments" were and how my "feelings" about always being thrust into positions of leadership and my not feeling "capable" had affected me over the years.

While this will be addressed another time and in another book, it drives home the point of this chapter. Your work ethic will be driven by the "attitude" you take towards responsibility.

However, please know that if God brings you to it, He has already equipped you to get you through it.

My purpose for sharing this is to encourage you to believe in yourself and your ability to rise to any decision, while keeping your focus on your why you are doing the work and what your desired outcome is.

With anything that you are assigned or choose to do, your love is to never be conditional, but your time is ALWAYS conditional.

When you are on your full-time job, you have a job description and your responsibilities are usually spelled out in minute detail. When you work on your dream, it's your time but you must still prioritize (covered in Chapter 7) and use your time wisely, but you don't have to do <u>everything</u>; thus the dollar on penny jobs.

From Chapter 3, where you used the **Weekly Plan Sheet,** use that tool to schedule time for the things (people) that are important to you.

## Five Tips for a Great Work Ethic

Attitude is EVERYTHING

Anything you're doing—Start on time; and end on time

Always do more than what is requested or required

Be solution conscious rather than problem conscious

Understand that not everyone desires to see you successful (we call them Haters); develop a thick skin and recognize and welcome constructive criticism, depending on the person's place in your life. If it is a leader, and/or someone you respect, take heed.

[If work is defined as activity involving mental and physical efforts done to achieve a purpose; and ethic is the science of morals/standards or behaviors concerning beliefs of what is or is not acceptable—then Work Ethic.]

## <u>Eight Practical Tips to Building</u>

Show up early—stay late.

Create and work off a check list. (Chapter 3)

Don't ask questions you can figure out on your own. (Be resourceful)

Always do more than you're asked! (Show initiative)

Never be doing nothing (Idle). (Offer to assist)

Don't complain about work at work! (Office politics gossip)

Turn complaints into suggestions for solutions. (Solution Conscious)

<u>Ignore the Haters!</u> (Develop a thick skin) (Respect-built)

In scripture, fruit is a metaphor used to describe the outward demonstration of one's inward disposition. Our fruit includes things like our behaviors, attitudes, words and thoughts. Fruit can be either good or bad.

Naturally, all people produce bad fruit (i.e., sinful actions, deeds or behaviors). Matthew 15:18-20; Romans 7:5; Galatians 5:22-24.

Our bad behaviors (fruits) is a natural result of being born with bad hearts (Psalm 51:5; Ephesians 2:3; Romans 5:12. Notice that it is not actions but qualities that have the priority. God first transforms our inner beings, which then results in our bearing good fruit outwardly.

# CHAPTER SEVEN

# Prioritize, Organize and Set Goals

*And whatever you do, do it heartily, as to the Lord, and not to men.*
COLOSSIANS 3:23 (AKJV)

This chapter is to be studied. In order to prioritize, organize and set goals, you must have what I call the "Big D" Discipline. Self-discipline (mastering you) is the ability to do what <u>should</u> be done <u>when</u> it should be done, whether you feel like it or not.

Renowned author and speaker Dr. John Maxwell says, "Time happens regardless of how we try to manage it." While it is impossible to manage time, we can maximize our time by instead managing our priorities. All of the principles shared in this book work, but nothing gets done if there is no discipline. Prioritizing is the foundation of organizing. With organized priorities, goal setting is inevitable and reaching those goals becomes real.

## **<u>Prioritize:</u>**

Your **Six Most Important Things List** is the way you prioritize. Use your five steps personalized bookmark that comes with this book to keep you on track. When you prioritize and use the list, even if you only get three or four of the things done, you got the most important things done that day. As the rule goes, move whatever wasn't closed to the top of the list for the next day. This is where another very important skill can/will be developed!

At the end of the week (or two), if there is something that keeps getting pushed to the bottom of the list or continually is not getting done, you may want to question its importance. Maybe it is, but YOU don't have to be the one who does it; in this case, delegate it (or dump it)! Developing the skill of delegation is a very powerful skill.

## **<u>Organize:</u>**

Organization is a personalized activity. We tend to organize the way we were taught or modeled. Many years ago, National Sales Director, Rena Tarbet, said in a training class I attended, "Some people organize in files and some organize in piles (piles of paper, etc.)." She was a very down to earth leader and comical but I identified with her right away because, at that time, I was a piler!!! "My files are organized," she said, "because I know exactly what's in them."

Over the years, I have used files (due to my teaching background and training in Business Education) but I often still use my "organized piles"—LOL (laughing out loud). I share this to say; find an organization system that works for you.

Depending on your profession, you may have someone who organizes for you, but you will want to develop a system that works well for your family.

If you happen to be a work-from-home person or run a homebased business, this information can be invaluable. Time is the most important commodity we have. "When we prioritize and organize, we make the most of our time. As the old saying goes, "Time is Money." With that in mind, Mary Kay taught, **"Don't spend dollar time on penny jobs"**.

When you are organizing and prioritizing and learning to delegate, I want to encourage every Kingdom Woman reading this book to consider the time you spend on the things you currently do. There will be many things that you do that are very important but do not have to be done by you. One of those things I personally feel is housekeeping.

Every woman I know wants a clean home, but if you're like me and really don't care for housework, my recommendation is "hire a maid!"

If you're reading this book, that tells me you're more than likely busy, right? Prayerfully, what you're busy doing is profitable! (Allow me to add a disclaimer here: If you are a stay-at-home mom or a mom who just loves housework, then please disregard that statement.)

However, if you are like me and figure that you are willing to pay those people who enjoy doing housework, then just think about it. When a person enjoys doing something, it's usually not work to them (to me it's literally hard labor).

When I was about 11 years old, I told my mother then that when I grew up I was going to have a housekeeper. So, you can imagine my excitement when in my first week of training in Mary Kay, I heard her say, "Hire a housekeeper!" I was literally living in an efficiency apartment, but I started then and have never regretted it. Over the years, I always taught my sales force leaders that concept, because it actually does free your mind (feelings) to work more effectively.

## **<u>Setting Goals:</u>**

*"Whatever it is you want to do in life is possible"* (Mark 9:23) but it must be planned. Goal setting can be defined as, "The development of an action plan designed to motivate and guide a person toward a desired result." You must have an end date to achieve your goals, but because it's <u>your</u> goal, the date can change but never the goal—if it's really something you want.

As a Kingdom Woman, I recommend you keep Matthew 6:33, *"Seek ye first the Kingdom of God and His righteousness and all these things will be added unto you,"* as your basic guide.

Putting God first, your family, then your career, will make all the difference. This is another principle I gleaned from my association with Mary

Kay Cosmetics. Because I always believed that my life is Divinely Led, becoming part of Mary Kay seemed a very natural next step, because that is how I lived; putting God first beforehand so it was very natural.

The discipline comes in when you master yourself to actually apply the principle. By the way, putting God first does not mean being in the building every time the church doors open, but living your life in a way that those who are looking on can see that the Spirit of God lives in you. Our first goal is to please God.

Proverbs 16:7 says, *"When a man's (mankind) ways please God, he makes even his enemies to be at peace with him."* That's exciting to me! Our goals will be in all areas of life, spiritual, family, career and personal, but follow the same steps: commit your goals to God.

Psalm 37:5 says, *"Commit thy way unto the Lord, trust also in him, and he shall bring it to pass."* Also see Proverbs 16:3.

## **Dream Big:**

God is a Big God and He said He would give us the desires of our hearts if we delight ourselves in Him. (Psalm 37:4).

It really is "ABOUT TIME"; time for us as Kingdom Women to walk in the fullness of what God has for us. Too often we are laden with too much to do and not enough time to do it.

When you apply these simple principles, desiring to please God, while you daily plan to be your best self, everyone and everything around you becomes better as you do it all to the Glory of God!!

# ABOUT THE AUTHOR

Bettye McCaskill Bridges is a teacher by calling and profession and has been deemed by her husband as the "ultimate optimist." She was born and raised in Mississippi in the early 1950's and graduated from Mississippi Valley State University with a Bachelor of Science Degree in Business and Office Administration.

Her career began in the mid 1970's as a business teacher at Dawson's Skills Center, an arm of Chicago City Colleges where she taught typing, shorthand, English and English as a Second Language (ESL).

During her time in Chicago, she pursued an on-the-side career in runway modeling and commercial voice-overs. While she enjoyed those fun adventures, her heart's desire was to be an entrepreneur.

She later went into retail sales at Baskins Clothiers for men in Oakbrook, IL and became the top salesperson writing over $25,000 per month. Her goal was to get experience in sales to one day become a buyer in the industry then start her own business. However, that was not to be.

From that position, she was offered the opportunity to become a Mary Kay Independent Beauty Consultant in February 1977. Reluctant because she didn't wear makeup, but when she heard you could win jewelry and earn a FREE car, she gave it a try! The rest, as they say, is history (or Herstory). Try it she did and, after earning over 36 years of FREE cars and 26 of those years Pink Cadillacs, she promoted herself to the highest position attainable in Mary Kay Cosmetics, Independent National Sales Director in April 2004.

The author is now a retired National Sales Director (Emeritus) and desires to share the experiences, lessons and wisdom gained as she literally "failed forward" to success. It is said that we learn "by precept and example." Her desire for this writing is that you will not have to endure many of the mistakes she made and arrive at your heart's desire sooner while wiser and more "fruitful!"

Bettye is married to Gerald and they have two adult children: Brandi-Bridges-Wheeler and Gerald Andrew Bridges. Three grandchildren: Mason Anthony Wheeler, Harper Elizabeth Wheeler, and Josiah Andrew Bridges.

To God be the Glory!

www.ingramcontent.com/pod-product-compliance
Lightning Source LLC
Chambersburg PA
CBHW070322160726
47999CB00003B/1109